ROCKED BY EARTHQUAKES

THERESE M. SHEA

PowerKiDS
press
New York

Published in 2018 by The Rosen Publishing Group, Inc.
29 East 21st Street, New York, NY 10010

First Edition

Editor: Melissa Ráe Shofner
Book Design: Reann Nye

Photo Credits: Cover, p. 1 Garry Gay/Photolibrary/Getty Images; pp. 4–30 (background) Claudiad/E+/Getty Images; pp. 4, 5 Antonio Nardelli/Shutterstock.com; p. 6 Nido Huebl/Shutterstock.com; p. 7 Peter Hermes Furian/Shutterstock.com; p. 9 mikluha_maklai/Shutterstock.com; p. 11 Encyclopaedia Britannica/Universal Images Group/Getty Images; p. 12 Clive Streeter/Dorling Kindersley/Getty Images; p. 13 jamesbenet/E+/Getty Images; p. 14 Bettmann/Getty Images; p. 15 PRAKASH MATHEMA/AFP/Getty Images; p. 17 KAZUHIRO NOGI/AFP/Getty Images; p. 18 Dutourdumonde Photography/Shutterstock.com; p. 19 Paula Bronstein/Getty Images News/Getty Images; p. 21 arindambanerjee/Shutterstock.com; p. 22 Perfect Gui/Shutterstock.com; p. 23 photka/Shutterstock.com; p. 24 Naypong/Shutterstock.com; p. 25 Justin Sullivan/Getty Images News/Getty Images; p. 27 https://commons.wikimedia.org/wiki/File:San_Francisco_Fire_Sacramento_Street_1906-04-18.jpg; p. 29 Pallava Bagla/Corbis News/Getty Images.

Library of Congress Cataloging-in-Publication Data

Names: Shea, Therese.
Title: Rocked by earthquakes / Therese M. Shea.
Description: New York : PowerKids Press, [2018] | Series: Natural disasters:
 how people survive | Includes index.
Identifiers: LCCN 2017019049| ISBN 9781538326527 (pbk. book) | ISBN
 9781538326534 (6 pack) | ISBN 9781538325636 (library bound book)
Subjects: LCSH: Earthquakes–Juvenile literature. | Natural
 disasters–Juvenile literature.
Classification: LCC QE521.3 .S53727 2018 | DDC 363.34/95–dc23
LC record available at https://lccn.loc.gov/2017019049

Manufactured in the United States of America

CPSIA Compliance Information: Batch #BW18PK: For Further Information contact Rosen Publishing, New York, New York at 1-800-237-9932

CONTENTS

IT'S A DISASTER!

"That was a disaster!" When people say this, they're usually talking about something that didn't go well. Maybe they failed a test or lost a game. They're often exaggerating, or stretching the truth, about what happened. A real disaster, however, is a sudden event that causes great damage and loss. Natural disasters are violent occurrences in nature. There are many kinds of natural disasters, including floods, wildfires, and earthquakes.

DISASTER ALERT!

We often think of how natural disasters affect people, but they can harm animals, too. They may also change landscapes forever.

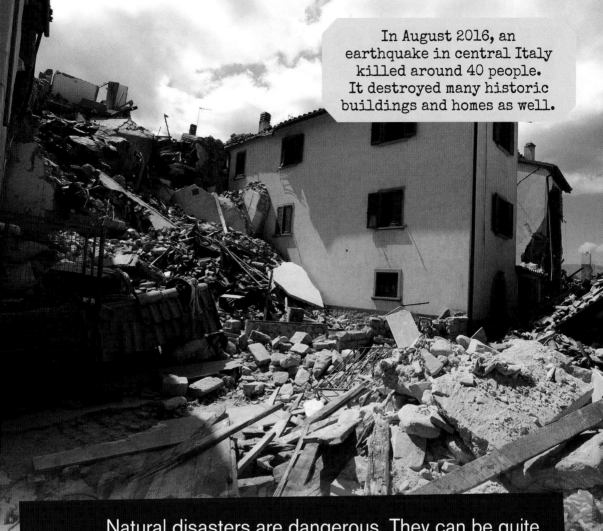

In August 2016, an earthquake in central Italy killed around 40 people. It destroyed many historic buildings and homes as well.

Natural disasters are dangerous. They can be quite sudden—and deadly. Earthquakes can't be prevented and are especially dangerous because they can't be **predicted**. Luckily, scientists have identified certain areas of the world where they're more likely to take place. In these regions, new **technology** has helped save people's lives and their property during earthquakes.

THE ORIGINS OF EARTHQUAKES

Most people know an earthquake causes the ground to shake, but they may not know the cause of this movement. Earth's outer shell, called the lithosphere, is made up of many large pieces of rock called tectonic plates. These plates float on a layer of hot, soft rock and are constantly in motion.

Visitors to Thingvellir National Park, Iceland, can walk in a space between the North American and Eurasian plates.

DISASTER ALERT!

Scientists call earthquakes "temblors."

JUAN DE FUCA PLATE

NORTH AMERICAN PLATE

EURASIAN PLATE

PACIFIC PLATE

PACIFIC PLATE

COCOS PLATE

CARIBBEAN PLATE

ARABIAN PLATE

INDIAN PLATE

PHILIPPINE PLATE

AFRICAN PLATE

NAZCA PLATE

SOUTH AMERICAN PLATE

AUSTRALIAN PLATE

ANTARCTIC PLATE

SCOTIA PLATE

The plates fit together like puzzle pieces, but they're not locked in place. Instead, they push against each other, pull apart, and slide past one another. The edges of these plates are called plate boundaries. They're uneven, and when two plate boundaries push on and slide past each other, they may catch on each other. Pressure builds as the plates try to keep moving. When the plates finally move, the pressure releases and an earthquake occurs.

A fault is a break in Earth's crust. Faults (and earthquakes) can also occur away from plate edges. Within a single plate, pieces can move in different directions. This means earthquakes can happen anywhere. When an earthquake occurs, the location above the fault, on Earth's surface, is called the epicenter.

An earthquake is felt in more locations than the fault and epicenter. Just as waves move through the ocean, waves of energy travel through the earth, shaking the ground—as well as everything connected to the ground—up and down and side to side. The pressure released at the fault moves outward in a form of energy called seismic waves. The most powerful earthquakes cause seismic waves that can be felt thousands of miles from the epicenter.

DISASTER ALERT!

Scientists think the fastest tectonic plate moves about 6 inches (15.2 cm) a year.

It's easy to see the fault line in this photo of exposed earth, but often the fault is deep beneath the surface.

fault line

Other Causes of Concern

Although the movements of tectonic plates and other blocks of earth cause most earthquakes, some earthquakes are caused by other sources. For example, liquid or partly liquid rock moving beneath a volcano can supply the pressure needed to produce changes in the crust, resulting in seismic waves. Small earthquakes have also occurred because of human activities. The pressure caused by large amounts of water held back by dams, underground nuclear explosions, and mine digging have all caused earthquakes.

WAVES OF ENERGY

Seismic waves that travel through the inner earth are called body waves. P, or primary, body waves squeeze and expand rock as they travel. S, or secondary, body waves move up and down or side to side, at right angles to the direction they travel. S waves are slower than P waves. Seismologists—scientists who study earthquakes—can tell how far away an earthquake began by comparing the arrival times of P and S waves.

An earthquake also produces other kinds of seismic waves called surface waves. These travel along the surface and cause the damage we see at ground level. The two kinds of surface waves are Love waves, which move from side to side, and Rayleigh waves, which move like a wave on the water, up and down and side to side.

DISASTER ALERT!

The fastest seismic wave, the P wave, moves 2.5 to 4.5 miles (4 to 7.2 km) per second!

These images show the force of each kind of seismic wave. P waves can travel through solids and liquids, but S waves can only travel through solids.

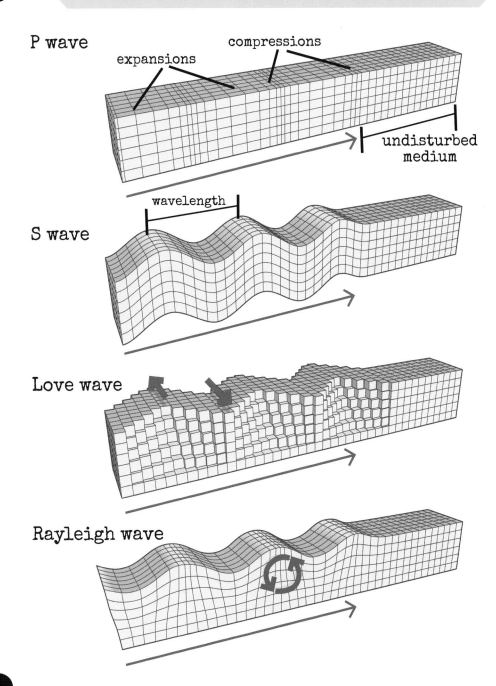

P wave

expansions

compressions

undisturbed medium

S wave

wavelength

Love wave

Rayleigh wave

11

SEISMOGRAPHS AND SEISMOGRAMS

Earthquakes are given a number depending on how big they are. Scientists figure out this measurement using an instrument called a seismograph. Simple seismographs have a base in the ground and a weight hanging from a spring. This weight is called a pendulum. When the ground shakes, the base shakes and the seismograph records the movement, sometimes on a sheet of paper. That record of the earthquake is a seismogram.

DISASTER ALERT!

A Chinese man named Zhang Heng made an early type of seismograph in AD 132! This shows that people have been concerned about earthquakes for a long time.

12

Modern seismographs like this electromagnetic instrument are sometimes called seismometers. They detect earthquakes that can't even be felt by people.

In a seismogram, a line with few waves means an earthquake was small, but a very wavy line means an earthquake was large. P waves are the first to be recorded on a seismogram, followed by S waves and then surface waves.

Most modern seismographs use electromagnets for more exact readings. Motions produce electric signals sent to a computer to create a seismogram.

13

The waves of a seismogram are used to calculate the strength of the earthquake. The most famous earthquake measurement scale is called the Richter magnitude scale. Scientists use the largest seismic wave on a seismogram to figure out a measurement called the magnitude. Earthquakes with a magnitude of 2.0 or less aren't usually felt by people. Those with magnitudes of 4.0 or less often don't cause much damage. Earthquakes with magnitudes of 6.0 or higher cause the most damage.

DISASTER ALERT!

An earthquake in Chile in 1960 was the largest ever recorded. Scientists believe it registered about 9.5 on the Richter scale.

The numbers of the Richter and moment magnitude scales usually match up closely, but the moment magnitude scale is thought to better capture the power of bigger quakes—those higher than 8.0 magnitude.

Many scientists today prefer to use the moment magnitude scale, which they think measures an earthquake's strength better. While the Richter scale uses the largest recorded wave for its measurements, a moment magnitude measurement reflects the total amount of energy released at a fault.

THE DEADLY DAMAGE

What kind of damage can a high-magnitude earthquake cause? Earthquakes can truly be disastrous, especially in highly populated areas. When buildings and bridges cannot withstand the shaking, they sink into softened ground or fall. People in and on these structures can be hurt or killed.

The trembling ground can also crack roads and railways, causing cars, trucks, and trains to turn off course. Another danger is the breaking of dams and **levees**, which hold back great amounts of water. The release of this water can cause flooding, property damage, and death by drowning.

Fire is another danger. When buildings, utility poles, and other structures are damaged, leaking natural gas lines and downed electrical wires can start fires. Damaged water pipes can slow efforts to put fires out.

Just as earthquakes can't be predicted, their terrible effects can't be predicted either.

Foreshocks and Aftershocks

Tremors are shaking movements before or after an earthquake. Those that happen before are called foreshocks. Until a larger quake occurs, scientists don't know that a tremor is a foreshock. Tremors that occur after an earthquake are called aftershocks. They may occur in the days, weeks, and months following a major quake.

17

Earthquakes don't just alter man-made structures—they can change natural landforms, too. In hilly areas with loose ground, seismic waves can cause landslides and mudslides. These can be **devastating** to communities in their path, even burying buildings and people.

Earthquakes under the ocean can cause giant waves called tsunamis. When these waves reach the shore, they can knock down buildings, flood towns and cities, and drown people. Earthquakes can even impact lakes. Lake waves called seiches (SAYSH-ehz) can knock down lakefront property and trees when they land.

Earthquakes can leave scars, or marks, across a landscape. Streams can change course when rocks move into their path or the land is altered in some other way. An earthquake can change a region forever.

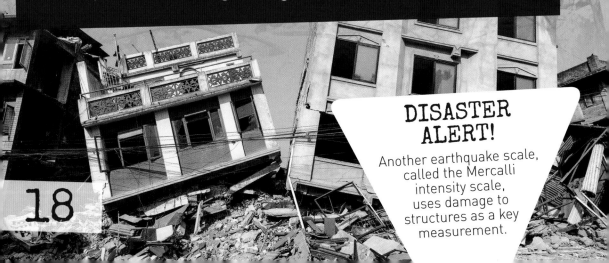

18

DISASTER ALERT!

Another earthquake scale, called the Mercalli intensity scale, uses damage to structures as a key measurement.

The earthquake that caused the Indian Ocean tsunami in 2004 was one of the most powerful in recorded history.

The Indian Ocean Tsunami

On December 26, 2004, an earthquake measuring 9.1 on the Richter scale occurred at the bottom of the Indian Ocean near the Indonesian island of Sumatra. Two hours later, gigantic waves, some as high as 30 feet (9.1 m), hit the coasts of India and Sri Lanka and, later, other islands. The tsunami killed at least 225,000 people across a dozen countries and sent waves as far as east Africa.

EMERGENCY EARTHQUAKE RESPONSE

In the hours after an earthquake, a quick response is important and can save lives. Local, state, national, and sometimes international response teams, including fire, medical, and rescue professionals, are swift to arrive. They look for survivors who may be trapped inside fallen buildings. They set up places where people can receive medical help if they need it. They help people find their missing loved ones. They may set up temporary shelters for people who have lost their homes. People also need clean water and food in the days following an earthquake.

Sometimes communities put together their own **emergency** response teams so they may spring into action before others can reach the scene. People on these teams are trained by professionals to assist their neighbors.

DISASTER ALERT!

After the first response, crews get to work clearing **debris** and taking down unstable structures.

The people of Haiti are still suffering years after the 2010 earthquake devastated their homes. As of 2016, tens of thousands were still living in tents.

Haiti Earthquake of 2010

On January 12, 2010, an earthquake occurred on the island of Hispaniola, home to the countries of Haiti and the Dominican Republic. It did terrible damage, especially to Haiti, because the structures there weren't built to withstand seismic forces. The buildings fell, trapping, injuring, and killing many people. Estimates of the number of people killed range from 80,000 to over 300,000. Rescue efforts were slowed by blocked roads and downed power and communication lines.

EARTHQUAKE PREPAREDNESS

Scientists aren't able to predict exactly where and when an earthquake will occur. They know where earthquakes are likely to happen because of past earthquakes and tectonic plate movement. However, earthquakes can happen anywhere, so it's important to be prepared for them and other emergencies.

DISASTER ALERT!

Vibrations, or small rapid movements, can be detected right before an earthquake occurs. At that point, however, it's too late to warn people.

Make an emergency kit with a first-aid kit for injuries, a battery-powered radio to hear news, and a flashlight and extra batteries in case of a loss of power. To prepare your house for an earthquake, make sure there are no heavy objects on shelves. These and other pieces of furniture can be anchored to walls and floors so they're less likely to move. You and your family should talk about a good place to meet in case you're separated during an earthquake.

It's good to have bottled water and food that won't spoil in your emergency kit. Sometimes harmful bacteria get into the public water supply after earthquakes and other natural disasters, making the water unsafe to drink.

What do you do if an earthquake strikes? First, don't panic. Stay wherever you are until the shaking stops. If you're indoors, stay near the center of the building near a wall, where the structure is strongest. Get to your hands and knees and cover your head and neck. You could also crawl under a table that could support weight if something fell on top of it. Don't stay near windows and doors or near things that could fall on you, such as lights.

DISASTER ALERT!

If you're in a car when an earthquake strikes, stop and stay inside it. Drivers should avoid stopping near trees or buildings or on bridges.

Many schools practice drills to keep students safe in case an earthquake strikes while they're in the building. Does your school have a plan?

If you're outside, stay away from power lines, poles, trees, buildings, and other structures that could fall. Drop to all fours and cover your head and neck. If you're in a city, it may be best to enter a building to avoid the many dangers outside.

ENGINEERING FOR EARTHQUAKES

Most of the danger to people during an earthquake comes from man-made structures collapsing. Though some **engineers** and **architects** claim they can build an earthquake-proof building, the costs of such a structure would be very high. Instead, they work to build earthquake-resistant structures in places that have experienced earthquakes in the past. They plan buildings to be **symmetrical** so that no part of the structure is weaker than another. They don't include decorations that could easily fall and harm people.

Engineers also use materials with high ductility when building in areas that tend to have earthquakes. Ductility is the ability to stretch or change shape without breaking. Materials such as brick and concrete have low ductility. However, steel has high ductility, allowing buildings, bridges, and other structures to bend.

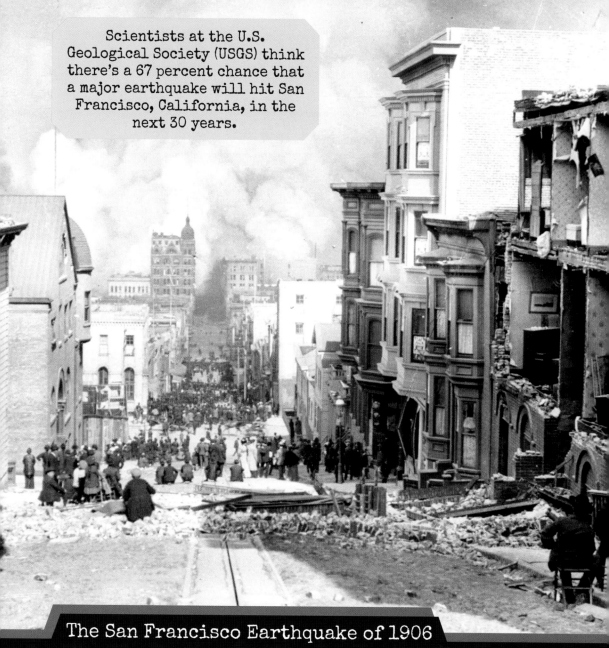

Scientists at the U.S. Geological Society (USGS) think there's a 67 percent chance that a major earthquake will hit San Francisco, California, in the next 30 years.

The San Francisco Earthquake of 1906

California has experienced many powerful earthquakes over the years. On April 18, 1906, an earthquake occurred off the coast of Northern California early in the morning. People in San Francisco later described a terrible roaring noise as the city shook and buildings collapsed. It's believed that about 3,000 people died and 250,000 people lost their homes. Much of the city was rebuilt to be

Earthquake-resistant buildings need to withstand seismic waves. Within a building, special structural systems, such as **diaphragms**, are placed in the floors and roof. When the building experiences a horizontal, or sideways, force, the diaphragms work with vertical structures to withstand it. **Diagonal** pieces called trusses may strengthen diaphragms. To strengthen the vertical structure of a building, engineers use trusses in frames, sometimes crossing them to make an "X" shape. Shear walls are stiff, vertical walls that resist forces that would make a building rock.

All these earthquake-resistant features can be used together in a building to combat structural collapse. Until we can really build earthquake-proof buildings, engineers and architects will work to create the safest possible buildings to save lives when the next earthquake strikes.

DISASTER ALERT!

Earthquake-resistant buildings may use springs and sliding joints to allow the building to move slightly with seismic activity.

Engineers have found ways to make soil beneath buildings stronger. They can also drive piles, or building supports, deep into the earth. This building in India has piles that are nearly 200 feet (61 m) deep!

More Earthquake-Resistant Ideas

Since buildings may separate from their foundation during an earthquake, some earthquake-resistant buildings use base isolation. This means "floating" a building on top of its foundation, connecting it through springs, **bearings**, or padded **cylinders**. When an earthquake hits, the foundation moves, but there's less movement in—and less damage to—the building above. Another idea is a rocking frame, which uses steel frames and cables. When seismic waves arrive, the frame rocks, but the structure doesn't collapse.

EARTHQUAKE SAFETY TIPS

The danger isn't over after an earthquake. Follow these tips to stay safe:

- Expect aftershocks.

- Check yourself and the people you're with for injuries. Don't move injured people. Provide first aid if possible.

- Leave the building if it seems unstable.

- Don't touch fallen power lines.

- Be careful around broken glass and other debris.

- Stay away from coastal areas in case of tsunamis.

- If you're trapped, use a cell phone to call for help. If you don't have a phone, make noise so others can find you.

- Don't light candles in case gas lines are broken. Use a flashlight.

- If you're at school, follow instructions closely.

- At home, listen to news on a battery-powered radio to find out what you should do next.

GLOSSARY

architect: A person who designs, or plans, buildings.

bearing: A machine part in which another part turns or slides.

cylinder: An object shaped like a tube.

debris: Broken pieces of objects.

devastating: Causing great damage or harm.

diagonal: Joining two opposite corners of a shape, especially by crossing the center point of the shape.

diaphragm: A horizontal system in a structure that acts to spread forces to vertical-resisting parts.

emergency: An unexpected situation that needs quick action.

engineer: Someone who uses math and science to do useful things, such as build machines.

levee: A long wall of soil built along a river to prevent flooding.

predict: To guess what will happen in the future based on facts or knowledge.

symmetrical: Having sides or halves that are the same.

technology: A method that uses science to solve problems and the tools used to solve those problems.

INDEX

WEBSITES

Due to the changing nature of Internet links, PowerKids Press has developed an online list of websites related to the subject of this book. This site is updated regularly. Please use this link to access the list: www.powerkidslinks.com/natd/quake